Knitted Sweater Patterns

The 10 Easiest Sweaters to Knit

Copyright © 2022

All rights reserved.

Contents

What is the difference between a sweater and a knitted sweater?

Knitwear can be divided into two categories: cotton knitwear and wool knitwear. Wool knitwear is commonly known as "sweater" which includes wool, cashmere, chemical fiber or wool blend knitwear.

So a sweater is a kind of knitted sweater and knitted sweater is a broader general term.

Knitted sweaters are made using knitting equipment. The raw materials for knitted sweaters include cotton yarn and various chemical fiber yarns in addition to wool.

The processing methods of cotton knitwear and wool knitwear are also different. Cotton knitwear has cutting and sewing processes while wool knitwear does not have these two processes and the pieces of clothing need to be put together by sewing plates.

Sweaters are made by using knitting equipment (computerized flat knitting machines) to form loops of wool and then string them over each other; knit them into front pieces, back pieces, sleeves, collars, patches, etc and then sew them into garments through the sewing plate process.

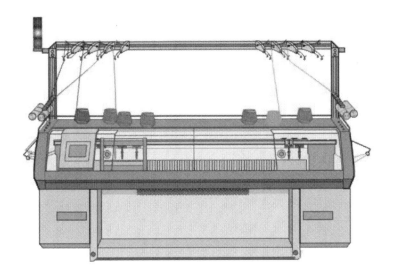

Sweaters can be roughly divided into two categories.

1. Thicker sweaters which are mainly for autumn and winter styles; see the following pictures.

2. Thinner sweaters which are mainly for spring and summer styles. Examples can be some simple cardigans which are generally called knitted shirts, summer knitted short-sleeves, knitted suspenders, knitted dresses, etc.

The 10 Easiest Sweaters to Knit

1. Simple Sweater

Designed by Ashleigh Kiser aka Sewrella, this Simple Knit Sweater the project for a first time pullover. It's knitted in pieces from the bottom up and then seamed together. The body is worked in garter stitch (knit every row) on chunky yarn so you can make a sweater in a weekend.

Knitted Sweater Patterns

Materials:

- Lion Brand Yarn Wool Ease Thick & Quick in Fisherman (XS-S: 5 skeins, M-L: 6 skeins, XL-2XL: 7 skeins, 3XL: 8 skeins)
- Size 17/12mm knitting needles (I love using the Takumi Bamboo circular needles with a 24" cord from Clover USA)
- Large eye tapestry needle
- Stitch markers

Gauge:

- 8 sts in garter stitch = 4 in.
- 16 rows = 4 in.

Measurements:

- Bust: 30" (XS) 34" (S) 38" (M) 42 " (L) 46" (XL) 50" (XXL) 54" (XXXL)
- Width across back: 17" (XS) 18" (S) 19" (M) 20" (L) 21" (XL) 22" (XXL) 23" (XXXL)
- Length: 21" (XS) 22" (S) 23" (M) 23.5" (L) 24" (XL) 24.5" (XXL) 24.5" (XXXL)

- Armhole: 6" (XS) 6.5" (S) 6.5" (M) 7" (L) 7" (XL) 7.5" (XXL) 8" (XXXL)
- Sleeve Length: 16.5" (XS) 17" (S) 17" (M) 17.5" (L) 17.5" (XL) 18" (XXL) 18" (XXXL)

Abbreviations:

- co – cast on
- k – knit
- k2tog – knit 2 stitches together
- p – purl
- rep – repeat
- rs – right side
- st(s) – stitch(es)
- ws – wrong side

Pattern Notes:

- Difficulty level: 1/Beginner
- For reference, model is 5'5" tall, and wearing the Simple Knit Sweater in a size Medium. Fit is oversized, for a more fitted sweater size down.

Knitted Sweater Patterns

- Sizing listed in the pattern will be in X-Small with Small, Medium, Large, Xl, 2X, and 3X listed in parenthesis such as 36 "(41, 46, 51, 56, 61, 66)" whereas co 36 for size XS, 41 for size S, 46 for size M, 51 for size L, 56 for size XL, 61 for size 2X and 66 for size 3X. When only one number is given, it applies to all sizes. To follow pattern more easily, circle/highlight all numbers pertaining to your size before beginning.

- This pullover sweater is worked in 5 pieces, the front and back panels, 2 sleeve panels then seamed together. The neckline ribbing is stitched on last by picking up stitches.

Simple Knit Sweater

Back Panel

- Co 30 (38, 46, 54, 62, 70, 78) sts

- Ribbing

- Rows 1 – 6: K1, P1, rep across

- Body

- Rows 7 – 58 (62, 66, 70, 74, 78, 82): K all sts (garter st)

- Bind off all sts

Front Panel

- Co 30 (38, 46, 54, 62, 70, 78) sts

- Ribbing

- Rows 1 – 6: K1, P1, rep across

- Body

- Rows 7 – 52 (56, 60, 64, 68, 72, 76): K all sts (gater st)

Shoulder shaping

Row 1: K 9 (12, 15, 18, 21, 24, 27) sts, bind off 12 (14, 16, 18, 20, 22, 24) sts for the neckline, K remaining 9 (12, 15, 18, 21, 24, 27) sts for the other shoulder

Row 2: K all sts on one shoulder side (first 9, 12, 15, 18, 21, 24, 27 sts), leave remaining sts on the needle unworked (finish one shoulder at a time)

Row 3: K2tog, K all remaining sts on that shoulder side

Row 4: K all sts

Row 5: Repeat Row 3

Bind off all sts on that shoulder side

Join yarn to other shoulder side (close to neckline) and K all sts

Row 2: K all sts

Row 3: K2tog, K remaining sts

Row 4: K all sts

Row 5: Repeat Row 3

Bind off all sts

Weave ends.

Sleeves

*make 2

Co 26 (28, 30, 32, 36, 38, 40) sts

Rows 1 – 32: K all sts (garter st)

Row 33: K 3, K2tog, rep across

Rows 34 – 54 (56, 56, 58, 58, 60, 60): K all sts

Ribbing

Rows 1-6: K1, P1, rep across

Bind off all sts

Seaming

Shoulder seams: Sew front shoulder shaping with a mattress stitch to back panel with WS facing you.

Sleeve: Open your sweater with seamed shoulders to lie flat with RS facing up. Lie sleeves flat with RS facing up. Count to center of sleeve Co sts, match up with shoulder seam and place a stitch marker to hold centered in place. Sew sleeve's Co edge to sweater bodice with a whip stitch. Repeat on other side.

Side seams: Fold sweater to match the side seams and sleeve underarm seam. Sew with an invisible vertical seam beginning with sleeve ribbing, along underarm, and continuing along the front and back panel body and finish with bodice ribbing. Repeat on other side

Weave all ends.

Neckline

Pick up stitches all along the neckline of the sweater (working into the shoulder seams themselves and all cast off stitches).

# of neckline stitches will vary depending on your size, just make sure you've picked up an even number of stitches.

Rows 1-2: K 1, P 1, rep around

Bind off all sts

Weave all ends.

2. Tweedy Stripey Pullover

Tweedy Stripey was designed by Leslie Weber and it's a free pattern.

It's a very simple, boxy pullover with no shaping and wide neckline.

It uses a tweed yarn which is on trend for the season.

A square-bodied pullover intended to be worn with approximately ten inches / 25 cm of positive ease. Your imagination is the limit for colour combinations in stripes or colour blocks.

The pattern is written for one size only: chest and hip circumference 46" / 117 cm, length 24" / 61 cm. Suggestions for re-sizing are given, and all measurements are indicated in rows as well as inches and cm on the schematic. (Many knitters may wish to pay particular attention to the sleeve width.)

The original sweater was made with a discontinued yarn. Suggestions for substitute heavy DK or light worsted yarns are provided.

Yarn quantities for original size: Colour A (light grey in photos) 369 yds / 338 m; Colour B (dark grey) 246 yds / 225 m; Colour C (brown) 523 yds / 478 m.

Construction:

Back and front are worked separately and joined at shoulders with a 3-needle bind-off. Stitches are picked up and worked in the round for neck trim. Stitches are picked up for sleeves and worked flat to lower edge. Underarm and side seams are worked in mattress stitch.

Please note that the pattern as written is for a very simple, boxy pullover with no body shaping and a fairly wide neckline. Personal fitting, adjustments and yarn choice are left to the knitter's discretion, as noted above. Some of the projects shown here incorporate custom details (longer "shirt tail" at the back, ribbed or garter stitch hem or cuffs, different neck width or sleeve length, very skinny sleeves...) which are the knitters' own modifications. And yes, one project was machine-knitted!

Skill level:

For the instructions as written -- some familiarity with following garment patterns.

For a re-sized version -- experience in making major modifications to a pattern.

3. 80-20 Time Out Cardigan

Knit a longer length cardigan with long sleeves and a shawl collar. This free pattern is compliments of Drops Design.

Knitted Sweater Patterns

Sizes: S - M - L - XL - XXL

Finished measurements:

Bust: 82-94-102-114-126 cm [32.25" - 37" - 40 1/8" - 44 7/8" - 49 5/8"]

Hem: 92-102-108-120-132 cm [36.25" - 40 1/8" - 42.5" - 47.25" - 52"]

Materials: Drops Angora-Tweed from Garnstudio

400-400-450-500-550 gr nr 06, brown and use: Drops Vivaldi from Garnstudio

200-200-250-250-250 gr nr 02, brown

Or use: Drops Lima from Garnstudio

600-600-650-750-800 gr nr 5310, light brown and use: Drops Brushed Alpaca Silk from Garnstudio

200-200-250-250-250 gr nr 05, beige

DROPS 7 mm [US 10½] needles, or size needed to obtain correct gauge.

Knitted Sweater Patterns

Instructions

Gauge: 14 sts x 17 rows with 1 strand of each yarn in stockinette st = 10 x 10 cm.

Rib: * K 4, P 4 *, repeat from * - *.

Back: Cast on loosely 66-74-78-86-94 sts with 1 strand of each yarn. Knit 2 rows garter st. Then knit rib as follows

Row 1 (right side):

Size S: K 1 (edge st knit in garter st) and K 2, * P 4, K 4 *, repeat from * - * to the last 7 sts, P 4, K 2, K 1 (edge st knit in garter st).

Size M: K 1 (edge st knit in garter st) and P 2, * K 4, P 4 *, repeat from * - * to the last 7 sts, K 4, P 2, K 1 (edge st knit in garter st).

Size L and XXL: K 1 (edge st knit in garter st), K 4, * P 4, K 4 *, repeat from * - *, finish with K 1 (edge st knit in garter st).

Size XL: K 1 (edge st knit in garter st) and P 4, * K 4, P 4 *, repeat from * - *, finish with K 1 (edge st knit in garter st).

When the rib measures 4 cm change to stockinette st. When the piece measures 15 cm dec 1 st at each side every 12-12-20-20-20 cm a total of 3-3-2-2-2

times = 60-68-74-82-90 sts.

When the piece measures 52-53-54-55-56 cm bind off for armhole at each side every other row: 3 sts 0-1-1-1-1 time, 2 sts 1-0-1-2-4 times and 1 st 1-4-4-5-4 times = 54-54-56-58-60 sts.

When the piece measures 65-67-69-71-73 cm bind off the center 26-26-28-28-28 sts for the neck. Then bind off at each neck edge every other row: 3 sts 1 time, 2 sts 1 time and 1 st 3 times = 6-6-6-7-8 sts remain on each shoulder. Bind off when the piece measures 71-73-75-77-79 cm.

Right front: Cast on 20-24-26-30-34 sts with 1 strand of each yarn and knit 2 rows garter st, then knit rib as follows (beginning of row is center front edge):

Row 1 (right side):

Size S: K 1 (edge st knit in garter st), * K 4, P 4 *, repeat from * - * 2 times, K 2, K 1 (edge st knit in garter st) .

Size M: K 1 (edge st knit in garter st), K 4, * P 4, K 4 *, repeat from *

- * 2 times, P 2, K 1 (edge st knit in garter st) .

Size L: K 1 (edge st knit in garter st), * K 4, P 4 *, repeat from * - * 3 times, K 1 (edge st knit in garter st).

Size XL: K 1 (edge st knit in garter st), K 4, * P 4, K 4 *, repeat from * - * 3 times, K 1 (edge st knit in garter st).

Size XXL: K 1 (edge st knit in garter st), * K 4, P 4 *, repeat from * - * 4 times, K 1 (edge st knit in garter st).

When the piece measures 4 cm change to stockinette st, keeping 1 edge st at each side in garter st. When the piece measures 15 cm dec 1 st at the side every 12-12-20-20-20 cm a total of 3-3-2-2-2 times = 17-21-24-28-32 sts.

Neckband: When the piece measures 46-48-50-52-54 cm dec 1 st at center front edge for neckband every 4 rows 8-8-9-9-9 times.

When the piece measures 52-53-54-55-56 cm bind off for armhole at the side as on back = 6-6-6-7-8 sts remain on shoulder. When the piece measures 71-73-75-77-79 cm bind off all sts.

Left front: Cast on and knit the same as the right front, reversing all

Knitted Sweater Patterns

shaping.

Sleeve: Cast on loosely 34-34-42-42-42 sts with 1 strand of each yarn and knit 2 rows garter st, then knit rib for 18 cm, keeping 1 edge st at each side in garter st. Then knit stockinette st to finished measurements. After the rib inc 1 st at each side every 4-3.5-4.5-3-2.5 cm a total of 8-9-7-9-10 times = 50-52-56-60-62 sts. When sleeve measures 51-49-48-46-44 cm bind off for sleeve cap at each side every other row: 4 sts 1 time, 3 sts 1 time, 2 sts 1-1-1-1-0 time and 1 st 0-1-2-4-7 times, then bind off 2 sts at each side until the piece measures 56 cm, then bind off 3 sts at each side 1 time. The piece measures approx. 57 cm, bind off the remaining sts.

Assembly: Sew shoulder seams.

Buttonband and collar: Pick up with 1 strand Angora-Tweed + 1 strand Vivaldi starting at lower edge on right front and up to center back: 120-124-128-132-136 sts (divisible by 4). K 1 row from wrong side and then K 1 row from right side. Knit the next row as follows (begin row at center back) = wrong side:

Sizes S, L and XXL: K 2, * P 4, K 4 *, repeat from * - *, finish with P 4 and K 2 (edge sts knit in garter st at lower edge).

Sizes M and XL: P 2, * K 4, P 4 *, repeat from * - *, finish with K 2 (edge sts in garter st at lower edge).

Continue the rib as established – from the right side the buttonband starts with K 2 (edge sts knit in garter st) and K 4 from lower edge.

When buttonband measures 10 cm inc 1 st in the center of the first three P 4 ribs from center back edge (seen from the right side) = 123-127-131-135-139 sts. When the piece measures 14 cm inc 1 st in the center of each of the first three K 4 ribs from center back (seen from the right side) = 126-130-134-138-142 sts. When the collar measures 24 cm K 1 row from right side, increasing 8 sts evenly distributed over top 30 sts at back of the neck. Then K 1 row from wrong side and bind off.

Repeat along left front.

Sew the collar at center back. Sew in sleeves. Sew sleeve and side seams using edge sts as a seam allowance.

Belt: Cast on 9 sts with 1 strand of each yarn. Knit rib = K 1, P 1, keeping 1 st in garter st at each side. Bind off in rib when belt measures approx. 120-140 cm.

Tube hat and wristwarmers:

Sizes: One-size

Materials: Garnstudio ANGORA-TWEED

70% merino wool, 30% angora, 50 g/145 m/158 yds

100 gr nr 06, brown

Drops 4.5 mm [US 7] needles, or size needed to obtain correct gauge.

Gauge: 20 sts x 40 rows garter st = 10 x 10 cm.

Tube Hat: Cast on 36 sts and knit garter st until the piece measures 44 cm, bind off. Sew cast-on edge and bind-off edge to each other so that it forms a tube, approx. 18 cm.

Wristwarmers: Cast on 30 sts. Knit garter st until the piece measures 18 cm, bind off. Sew cast-on edge and bind-off edge to each other so that it forms a tube, approx. 15 cm. Knit a second wristwarmer.

Knitted Sweater Patterns

Diagram

All measurements in charts are in cm.

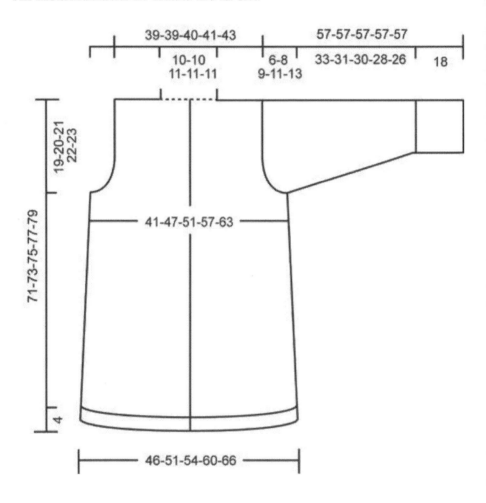

4. Lacy Knitted Sweater

Materials

#3 Light weight yarn

Ice Yarn Organic Baby Cotton in color Ecru #3 Light weight yarn

Needles size: US 6/4mm knitting needles (You can use straight or circular needles)

Scissors

Yarn needle

Stitch markers

*These materials contain affiliate links, for which I make a small commission. It's no extra cost to you, makes shopping easier and helps to keep the lights on.

Stitches Used & Code

CO = Cast on

BO = Bind off

K = Knit

P = Purl

Knitted Sweater Patterns

P2tog = Purl 2 st together

YO = Yarn over

ST = Stitch(es)

REP = Repeat

RS = Right side

WS = Wrong side

” = Inches

Skill: Easy

Notes:

The pattern is written in English US terminology

The pattern is made as US women's sizes XS(S, M, L, XL, XXL)

In this picture I have demonstrated with size Small

This pattern is knitted in row with 6 rows repeat (Row 12 – Row 17)

The pattern is made in 4 separate pieces and then sewn together (Front and back panels are made the same)

Yarn needed: 910(980, 1050, 1120, 1190, 1260) Yards

Gauge blocked: 20 st X 34 rows = 4" (in main stitch pattern)

- **Lacy Knitted Sweater Pattern**

Body Panel (Make 2)

Ribbing

CO 98(108, 118, 128, 138, 148) ST

Row 1 – Row 11: *K1, P1* REP from *TO* across. Total of 98(108, 118, 128, 138, 148) ST

Body

Row 12 – Row 16: K across (garter st). Total of 98(108, 118, 128, 138, 148) ST

Row 17 (WS): P1, *YO, P2tog* REP from *TO* until you have 1 st left, P the last st. Total of 98(108, 118, 128, 138, 148) ST

REP Row 12 – Row 17: 17(18, 19, 20, 21, 22) more times. You'll have a total of 119(125, 131, 137, 143, 149) rows, then BO all stitches. Cut the yarn and leave about 16-20" long tail

If you'd like a shorter or longer sweater, just REP row 12 – row 17 less or more times.

Sleeves (Make 2)

Ribbing

CO 62(68, 74, 80, 86, 92) ST

Row 1 – Row 11: *K1, P1* REP from *TO* across. Total of 62(68, 74, 80, 86, 92) ST

Sleeve body

Row 12 – Row 16: K across (garter st). Total of 62(68, 74, 80, 86, 92) ST

Row 17 (WS): P1, *YO, P2tog* REP from *TO* until you have 1 st left, P the last st. Total of 62(68, 74, 80, 86, 92) ST

REP Row 12 – Row 17: 20(20, 20, 20, 20, 20) more times. You'll have a total of 137(137, 137, 137, 137, 137) rows, then BO all stitches. Cut the yarn and leave about 40-60" long tail

For the sleeve all the sizes are the same length. If you'd like shorter or longer sleeves, just repeat row 12 – row 17 less or more times.

Join all the pieces together. Sew the back and front panels together

Take the back and front panels, place them with the correct side facing down, we'll sew in the wrong side using the tail that we left earlier. Sew 26(31, 35, 40, 44, 49) st of the front and back panel together at the shoulder seam. Use which ever method you prefer to sew (Both sides are sewn the same), if you'd like a smaller or bigger neck hole, you can sew more or less stitches from the shoulder seam. Just make sure both sides are even and the same number of stitches. (Check picture below)

Sew the sleeves to the main panel

With your main panel correct side facing down. Place your sleeves correct side facing down and start sewing on the wrong side with your tail again. The shoulder seam of the main panel should be in the middle of the sleeves panel and even on both sides. (Check picture below)

Sew the sweater together

Fold your sweater in half at the shoulder seam with the correct sides facing each other. Cut a new strand of yarn 60-70" long, enough to sew the side and the sleeve. Start sewing from the bottom up to the side seam until you reach the armpit and continue sewing the sleeve side seam all the way till the end, then weave all the ends (Check picture below)

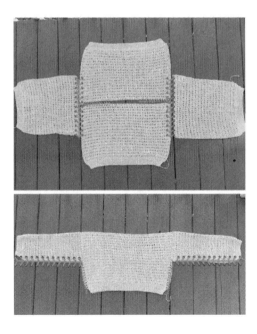

And that's it, you did it! Congratulations on your knitted sweater.

Wear it with pride because you know you made it with your own hands, hard work and dedication.

5. Chelsea Cape

Materials:

6 skeins Lion Brand 24/7 Cotton in Silver or approx. 1116yds/1020m of another worsted weight, cat. 4 yarn

Size US 10 (6mm) circular knitting needles, 29"/75cm or longer

Size US 10 (6mm) double pointed needles

Tapestry needle

Finished Size:

Width: 40"/102cm

Length: 44"/112cm

Gauge:

15 sts + 28 rows = 4"/10cm in pattern (unblocked)

12 sts + 24 rows = 4"/10cm in pattern (blocked)

Abbreviations:

All Two of Wands patterns are written in standard US terms

CO - Cast on

K - Knit

K2tog - Knit 2 together

P - Purl

Rep - Repeat

RS - Right side

Sl - Slip

St(s) - Stitch(es)

YO - Yarn over

Wyib - With yarn in back

Wyif - With yarn in front

Note: Reaching proper gauge for this project is important in order to achieve proper drape. Measure gauge before and after blocking. If it does not match you may need to adjust your needle size to reach it.

Wrap is worked side to side in a rectangle which is folded in half and seamed partly up the sides to form the armholes. All stitches are slipped purlwise. A ribbed selvedge edge is worked along the sides to make picking up stitches for the edging easier. Edging is created with an attached i-cord around body and armholes.

With circular needles, CO 131 sts.

Row 1 (RS): Sl 1 wyib, K 1, P 1, K to last 3 sts, P 1, K 2.

Row 2: Sl 1 wyif, P 1, K to last 2 sts, P 2.

Row 3: Sl 1 wyib, K 1, P 1, K to last 3 sts, P 1, K 2.

Row 4: Sl 1 wyif, P 1, K 1, *K2tog, YO, rep from * to last 4 sts, K 2, P 2.

Row 5: Sl 1 wyib, K 1, P 1, K to last 3 sts, P 1, K 2.

Row 6: Sl 1 wyif, P 1, K to last 2 sts, P 2.

Row 7: Sl 1 wyib, K 1, P 1, K to last 3 sts, P 1, K 2.

Row 8: Sl 1 wyif, P 1, K 2, *YO, K2tog, rep from * to last 3 sts, K 1, P 2.

Row 9: Sl 1 wyib, K 1, P 1, K to last 3 sts, P 1, K 2.

Row 10: Sl 1 wyif, P 1, K to last 2 sts, P 2.

Row 11: Sl 1 wyib, K 1, P 1, K to last 3 sts, P 1, K 2.

Rep rows 4-11 until work measures 34"/86cm when laying flat (unblocked).

Bind off. Block work. Fold in half horizontally so that the cast on and bind off edges are halved and the fold line is perpendicular to them. The piece should measure approx. 40"/102cm wide x 22"/ 56cm tall.

Seam up 14"/36cm on each side from the bottom edges up toward the fold line. The 8"/20cm spaces left un-seamed become the armholes.

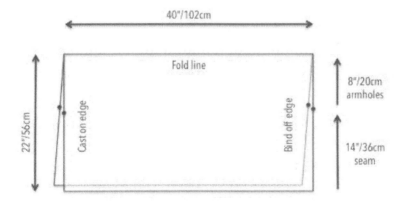

Edging:

Edging is created with an attached i-cord that is worked around the outer edge of the cape into the selvedge edge sts and around the armholes into the cast on and bind off sts.

Using two double pointed needles, CO 5 sts, leaving a long tail. Slide sts to other end of needle (working yarn will be at the bottom of the sts). Bring the yarn around the back and knit 4 sts. Slip the last st wyib purlwise.

Starting along the outer edge at one side seam with the right side of the fabric facing you, insert the needle containing the 5 sts into the first selvedge edge st to the left of the seam and pick up and knit a st into it. Pass the slipped st over the picked up st.

Slide the 5 sts to the other end of the needle. Bring the working yarn around the back, knit 4 sts, and slip the last st wyib purlwise. Pick up and knit a second st into the same selvedge edge st just worked in the last row, then pass the slipped st over it. Continue this process all the way around the outer edge of the cape. Each selvedge edge st will be worked into twice. Once you have gone all the way around the outer edge, graft the sts to the cast on edge of the i-cord using the long cast on tail.

To work the attached i-cord around the armholes, CO 4 sts, leaving a long tail. Slide sts to other end of needle (working yarn will be at the bottom of the sts). Bring the yarn around the back and knit 3 sts. Slip the last st wyib purlwise.

Starting along one armhole edge at the side seam with the right side of the fabric facing you, insert the needle containing the 4 sts into the first st to the left of the seam and pick up and knit a st into it. Pass the slipped st over the picked up st. Continue this process all the way around the armhole, working into each st only once this time. Once you have gone all the way around, graft the sts to the cast on edge of the i-cord using the long cast on tail. Repeat for other armhole.

Secure and weave in all ends.

6. Easy Knit Boxy T Shirt "Jeans" Pattern

Explanation:

This classic, comfortable, beginner friendly sweater is a breeze to make! If you know how to knit and purl, you will love making this roomy and soft knit t-shirt sweater. There's no need to know how to knit in the round and it works up quickly on large needles. Get ready to make this stylish piece that can be enjoyed year round.

Modeled on a size small. Pattern includes instructions for S, M, L, XL.

You will need:

US Size 15, 10.0 mm, 24" Circular Knitting Needles (You may use long straight needles if you're making a size small)

4 skeins (for a size small) of Lion Brand Yarn "Jeans" Faded worsted weight yarn (110 grams, 246 yards per skein) Small size uses 363 grams of yarn (Medium 5 skeins, Large 5 Skeins, XL 6 skeins – please purchase an extra skein as gauge may vary)

Scissors

Tapestry Needle to weave in ends

Abbreviations and Skills needed:

k- knit

p -purl

RS – right side

WS – wrong side

Gauge:

Approximately 2 ¾ stitches per inch and approximately 3.5 rows per inch

Determining Your Size:

Bust Size Circumference Approximation:

Small: 32" inches

Medium: 36" inches

Large: 40" inches

XL: 44" inches

Actual Sweater Size/Measurements:

*These are approximations. The sweater fabric is stretchy and flexible so the pattern is forgiving.

Notes: This sweater is made by making one front panel and one back panel. These panels are then seamed together to create the shirt. It is worked from the top down.

The fabric on this sweater is loose and stretchy.

This sweater is knit by holding two strands of yarn together at the same time.

You will follow the key throughout the pattern according to which size hat you are knitting.

Knit Boxy T Shirt Sweater Pattern:

Follow the key for your size (S, M, L, XL)

Holding two strands of yarn together, CO (88, 94, 100, 104) stitches

Row 1- 3 Knit across row

Once you've knit for three rows, you will begin the stockinette portion.

Stockinette Upper Sweater and Sleeve Portion:

Row 1 (RS): Knit Across row

Row 2 (WS): K4, purl across, knit last 4 stitches of row

Repeat rows 1 and 2 for a total of (30,32,33,35) rows

Once you've finished these rows, you will bind off for the sleeves.

Sleeve Bind Off

To create the bottom of the sleeve, you will cast off stitches from each end.

Bind off the first (21,22,23,23) stitches of the row, then knit or purl across depending on which side you are working (if the (RS) knit side is facing you, knit across. If the (WS) purl side is facing you, purl across) (46,50,54,58) stitches. Finally, bind off the last (21,22,23,23) stitches. Tie off and cut your yarn. You will now pick up the yarn to continue knitting the next section.

Mid to bottom portion

Pick up your yarn and continue to knit in stockinette stitch. If you ended on (WS) or purl row, you will now knit across. If you ended on the (RS) or knit row, begin by purling across the next row. Alternate these knit and purl rows for approximately (28,30,32,33) rows. Be sure to end on a purl row, meaning that your next row will be knit. This means you may need to add an extra row if you end on a knit row depending on which size you are knitting.

Bottom Ribbed Cuff

*Please note that the front panel of the sweater has a shorter ribbed

ection than the back panel.

Starting on the knit side or right side of the panel:

Row 1 (RS): K2, p2 across row

Row 2 (WS): purl across row

Repeat rows 1 & 2 for (front panel 2.5" inches, back panel 4" inches)

Tie off and weave in all ends

Repeat the pattern above in order to make the second panel of your top. There is a front and back panel. You will then seam then together.

Seaming:

Seam up sides:

With a length of yarn and your tapestry needle, you will seam up each side using the mattress stitch. Begin your seam just above the bottom ribbed portion of the sweater. Seam up the sides and under the arms.

Seam along top of sweater:

Seam in on each side of the top of the sweater with your preferred method, leaving a space in the center for your head and neckline. You may create shorter seams to have an off the shoulder look, or you may make your seams longer to have a smaller neckline. Pictured, the sweater is seamed 12" inches in on both sides for the size small. Weave in all ends and you're done!

7. Chunky Cable

Size Guide + Finished Measurements

Sizes written in 1 (2, 3, 4, 5) with a finished bust size of 35.5 (41, 46.5, 52, 58) in/ 90 (104, 118, 132, 147) cm. The cardigan has about 4-6 in/10-15 cm of positive ease so pick a sweater size accordingly. For example, if you're a 36 in/91.5 cm bust, a size 2 would be appropriate for about 5 in/12.5 cm positive ease. Sweater pictured is a size 2 on a 36 in/91.5 cm bust.

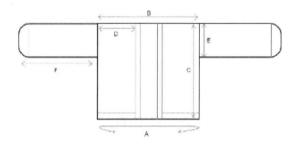

Size	A Bust Circumference	B Back Width	C Body Length
1	35.5 in/90 cm	18 in/45.5 cm	27 in/68.5 cm
2	41 in/104 cm	20.5 in/52 cm	27 in/68.5 cm
3	46.5 in/118 cm	23 in/58.5 cm	27 in/68.5 cm
4	52 in/132 cm	26 in/66 cm	31.5 in/80 cm
5	58 in/147 cm	29 in/73.5	31.5 in/80 cm

Size	D Front Panel Width	E Armhole Depth	F Sleeve Length
1	7 in/18 cm	7 in/18 cm	18 in/46 cm
2	8 in/20.5 cm	8 in/20.5 cm	18 in/46 cm
3	9 in/23 cm	9 in/23 cm	18.5 in/47 cm
4	10.5 in/26.5	9 in/23 cm	18.5 in/47 cm
5	11.5 in/29 cm	9.5 in/24 cm	19 in/48.5 cm

Note: Measurements are given for work unstretched and with minimal blocking made with 100% recycled polyester yarn. The cables tend to pull the cardigan together using synthetic yarn. I suggest using synthetic yarn for similar results. Using natural fiber will significantly change gauge, potentially adding 10 in/25.5 cm in width. Therefore, consider going down a size or two if knitting with natural fibers to accommodate the added width and length.

Yarn

Approximately 4 (4, 4, 5, 6) skeins of Lion Brand Re-Spun Thick + Quick (223 yds/204 m per 12oz/340g skein; 100% recycled polyester) or another super bulky weight yarn that meets gauge. Color shown is Whipped Cream.

Needles

Size 8mm (US11) 40 in/100 cm circular knitting needles for collar and sleeve cuff

Size 9mm (US13) 24 in/61 cm or longer circular knitting needles for back and sleeves

Or knitting needles required to obtain correct gauge.

Gauge

1 cable is 8 STS and 16 rows = 3 in/7.5 cm wide and 5 in/12.5 cm long

8. Sawtelle Adult

Craft: Knit

Skill Level: Easy

Project Type: Women's Clothing

Designer: Amanda Keep Williams

Sawtelle Adult cardigan is made entirely of knit sts and the only seaming is at the shoulders. It's the grown up version of our popular Sawtelle, for girls.

Shown in size Small

Sizes

Directions are for women's size X-Small. Changes for sizes Small, Medium, Large, 1X and 2X are in parentheses

Finished Measurements

Chest (closed) – 32(36-40-44-48-52)"

Length – 21½(22-23-23½-24½-25)"

Knitted Sweater Patterns

Materials

4(5-5-6-7-8) Balls Berroco Remix (100 grs), #3967 Bittersweet (MC) and

1 ball #3984 Ocean (CC)

Two 24" length circular knitting needles, size 8 (5.00 mm) OR SIZE TO OBTAIN GAUGE

2 St holders

1 St marker

Three 1" buttons

Gauge

17 sts = 4"; 32 rows = 4" in Garter St

17 sts = 4"; 23 rnds = 4" in St st

Note: Body of this garment is worked in one piece to the underarm, then divided for back and fronts. Shoulder seams are then sewn and sleeves are picked up and worked down in the round on 2 circular needles.

Body

With one circular needle, using CC, cast on 150(166-184-200-218-234) sts. DO NOT join. Work back and forth in Garter St for 3". Mark next row for RS of work. Change to MC and work even in Garter St until piece measures 13½(13½-14-14-14½-14½)" from beg, end on WS.

Divide for Armholes: Next Row (RS): K32(34-36-38-41-43), bind off 18(22-26-30-34-38) sts, k until there are 50(54-60-64-68-72) sts on RH needle after bound-off sts, bind off 18(22-26-30-34-38) sts, k to end.

Left Front: K32(34-36-38-41-43), slip next 50(54-60-64-68-72) sts onto holder for back, sl remaining 32(34-36-38-41-43) sts onto another holder for right front.

Work even until armhole measures 5½(6-6½-7-7½-8)", end on RS.

Shape Neck: Next Row (WS): Bind off 16(16-15-15-16-16) sts, k to end – 16(18-21-23-25-27) sts.

Dec Row (RS): K to last 3 sts, k2 tog, k1 – 15(17-20-22-24-26) sts. Rep this dec every RS row 3 times more – 12(14-17-19-21-23) sts. Work even until armhole measures 8(8½-9-9½-10-10½)", end on

VS. Bind off. Mark placement of 3 buttons on front edge, the first
" up from beg of armhole, the last ½" below beg of neck shaping and
he other evenly spaced between.

Back: With WS facing, join MC in first st on second holder. Using
circular needle, k50(54-60-64-68-72). Work even until armholes
measure 7½(8-8½-9-9½-10)", end on WS.

Shape Neck: Next Row (RS): K12(14-17-19-21-23), join another ball
of MC and bind off center 26 sts, k to end. Working both sides at
once, work even until armholes measure 8(8½-9-9½-10-10½)", end
on RS. Bind off.

Right Front: With WS facing, join MC in first st on remaining
holder. Using circular needle, k32(34-36-38-41-43). Work even until
armhole measures 1", end on WS.

Buttonhole Row (RS): K3, k2 tog, yo, k to end. Complete to
correspond to left front, reversing all shaping and making 2 more
buttonholes opposite markers on left front. Bind off for neck on RS
row. Work neck decs at beg of RS rows as k1, SSK. Sew shoulder
seams.

Sleeves

With RS facing, using one circular needle and MC, beg at center point of 18(22-26-30-34-38) bound-off sts at underarm, pick up and k34(36-38-40-42-44) sts to shoulder seam, using second circular needle, pick up and k34(36-38-40-42-44) sts to beg – 68(72-76-80-84-88) sts. Mark for beg of rnd and carry marker up. Work even in St st (k EVERY rnd) by knitting all the sts on first circular needle, then all the sts on second circular needle until sleeve measures 2" from beg. Note: Make sure when you start to knit each section that you pick up the other end of that needle to start knitting. If you pick up the end of the other needle, you will wind up with all the sts on one needle and will have to divide them onto 2 needles again.

Dec Rnd: K1, SSK, k to 3 sts before marker, k2 tog, k1 – 66(70-74-78-82-86) sts. Rep this dec every ¾" 16(18-19-21-22-24) times more – 34(34-36-36-38-38) sts. Work even until sleeve measures 20½" from beg. Change to CC and work even until sleeve measures 21" from beg. Bind off.

Finishing

Collar: With RS facing, using one circular needle and MC, beg at right front edge, pick up and k32 sts along right front neck edge, 28 sts across back neck edge, then 32 sts along left front neck edge – 92 sts. Work even in Garter St for 5", end on WS. Bind off. Sew on buttons.

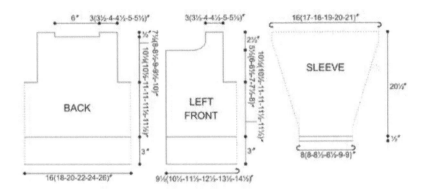

9. Two-Color Pullover

Knitted Sweater Patterns

Size:

XS/S (M/L, 1X/2X)

Finished Bust About 43 (50, 58)" (109 (127, 147.5) cm)

Finished Length About 19 (20, 21)" (48.5 (51, 53.5) cm)

Note: Pattern is written for smallest size with changes for larger sizes in parentheses. When only one number is given, it applies to all sizes. To follow pattern more easily, circle all numbers pertaining to your size before beginning.

Gauge:

13 sts + 18 rows = about 4" (10 cm) in St st (k on RS, p on WS).

Be sure to check your gauge.

Directions:

Notes:

Pullover is worked in 4 separate pieces: Back, Front and 2 Sleeves.

The Back is worked with yarn color A, Front is worked with yarn color B, and Sleeves are worked in intarsia colorwork with both yarn colors.

A circular needle is used to accommodate the number of stitches. Work back and forth in rows on the circular needle as if working on straight needles.

Stitches are picked up along the neck edge for the neckband, then neckband is worked in two halves using one color of yarn for each half.

Back:

With A, cast on 70 (82, 94) sts.

Row 1 (RS): P2, *k2, p2; rep from * across.

Row 2: K the knits sts and p the purl sts.

Rep Row 2 until piece measures about 2" (5 cm) from beg, end with a WS row as the last row you work.

Beg with a RS (knit) row, work in St st (k on RS, p on WS) until piece measures about 19 (20, 21)" (48.5 (51, 53.5) cm) from beg, end with a RS row as the last row you work.

Last Row (WS): Bind off first 21 (25, 29) sts for left shoulder, purl until there are 28 (32, 36) sts on the right hand needle and slip these sts onto a holder for back neck, bind off rem sts for right shoulder.

Front:

With B, cast on 70 (82, 94) sts.

Row 1 (RS): (P2, k2) 5 (6, 7) times, p1, place marker (pm), k28 (32, 36), sm, p1, (k2, p2) 5 (6, 7) times.

Row 2: K the knit sts and p the purl sts to first marker, slip marker (sm), k to next marker, sm, k the knit sts and p the purl sts to end of row.

Rep Row 2 until piece measures about 2" (5 cm) from beg, end with a WS row as the last row you work.

Next Row (RS): Knit, slipping markers as you come to them.

Next Row: P to first marker, sm, k to next marker, sm, p to end of row.

Rep last 2 rows until piece measures about 19 (20, 21)" (48.5 (51, 53.5) cm) from beg, end with a RS row as the last row you work.

Last Row (WS): Bind off first 21 (25, 29) sts for right shoulder, knit until there are 28 (32, 36) sts on needle and place these sts on a holder for front neck, bind off the rem sts for left shoulder.

Right sleeve:

With A, cast on 29 (31, 33) sts; then with B, cast on 29 (31, 33) sts for a total of 58 (62, 66) sts.

Sizes XS/S (1X/2X) ONLY

Row 1 (RS): With B, (k2, p2) 7 (8) times, k1; with A, k1, (p2, k2) 7 (8) times.

Row 2: Working A-colored sts with A and B-colored sts with B, k the knit sts and p the purl sts.

Rep Row 2 until piece measures about 17" (43 cm) from beg.

Bind off A-colored sts with A and B-colored sts with B.

Size M/L ONLY

Row 1 (RS): With B, (k2, p2) 7 times, k2, p1; with A, p1, k2, (p2, k2) 7 times.

Row 2: Working A-colored sts with A and B-colored sts with B, k the knit sts and p the purl sts.

Rep Row 2 until piece measures about 17" (43 cm) from beg.

Bind off A-colored sts with A and B-colored sts with B.

Left sleeve:

With B, cast on 29 (31, 33) sts; then with A, cast on 29 (31, 33) sts for a total of 58 (62, 66) sts.

Sizes XS/S (1X/2X) ONLY

Row 1 (RS): With A, (k2, p2) 7 (8) times, k1; with B, k1, (p2, k2) 7 (8) times.

Row 2: Working A-colored sts with A and B-colored sts with B, k the knit sts and p the purl sts.

Rep Row 2 until piece measures about 17" (43 cm) from beg.

Bind off A-colored sts with A and B-colored sts with B.

Size M/L ONLY

Row 1 (RS): With A, (k2, p2) 7 times, k2, p1; with B, p1, k2, (p2, k2) 7 times.

Row 2: Working A-colored sts with A and B-colored sts with B, k the knit sts and p the purl sts.

Rep Row 2 until piece measures about 17" (43 cm) from beg.

Bind off A-colored sts with A and B-colored sts with B.

Neckband

Sew right shoulder seam.

Slip the 28 (32, 36) back neck sts and 28 (32, 36) front neck sts from the holders back onto the circular needle so that you are ready to work a RS row – you will have a total of 56 (64, 72) sts on the needle.

Row 1 (RS): With B, k28 (32, 36) front sts; with A, k28 (32, 36) back sts.

Rows 2-16: Working A-colored sts with A and B-colored sts with B, work in Garter st (k every st on every row).

Bind off A-colored sts with A and B-colored sts with B.

Sew left shoulder, including neckband.

Finishing:

Place markers on side edges of Front and Back, about 7 (7 1/2, 8 1/2)" (18 (19, 21.5) cm) below shoulder seams. Sew tops of Sleeves between markers.

Sew side and Sleeve seams.

Weave in ends.

Abbreviations:

beg = begin(ning)(s)

k = knit

p = purl

rem = remain(ing)(s)

rep = repeat

RS = right side

st(s) = stitch(es)

St st = Stockinette stitch

WS = wrong side

10. Folded Squares Cardigan

Materials

2 skeins of Habu's Dyed Bamboo, 100% bamboo. I used the color Silver.

US 4 (3.5 mm), 24, 32- or 47-inch circular needles

Please Note: Habu's Dyed Bamboo is no longer available but we recommend, instead, 3 (3, 4, 4, 4, 4) skeins of Purl Soho's Burnish, 100% rayon from bamboo. Each skein is 339 yards/ 100 grams; approximately 850, (930, 1090, 1180, 1275, 1375) required.

Gauge

Before blocking: 24 stitches and 44 rows = 4 inches in garter stitch

After blocking: 20 stitches and 36 rows = 4 inches in garter stitch

Stitch and row counts given in the pattern reflect final measurements after blocking.

Note: Whatever yarn you use to make this pattern, be sure to block your swatch and make sure you're getting the correct 'after blocking' gauge.

Sizes

Note: For help picking a size, please check out our Understanding Ease + Selecting Size Tutorial!

34 (38, 42, 46, 50, 54)

Finished Chest Circumference: 34 (38, 42, 46, 50, 54) inches

Length from Underarm to Bottom Edge: 9 (9, 9 ½, 9 ½, 9 ½, 9 ½) inches

Length from Underarm to Bottom Sleeve Edge: 6 ¾ (6 ¾, 7 ¼, 7 ¼, 7 ¼, 7 ¼) inches

Sample: Size 38

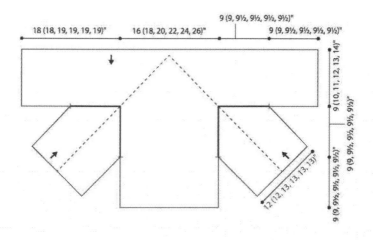

Notes

A garter stitch "ridge" is a horizontal corrugation formed by knitting two rows. Counting ridges is an easy way to determine how many rows you have knit without having to count as you work. If you find this confusing, just multiply the number of ridges given by two, and that is how many rows you should knit. For example, 40 ridges is 80 rows.

Bind off all stitches as follows: *K2tog tbl (through the back loop), place stitch back on left needle, repeat from *.

Pattern

Fronts and back

Cast on 260 (270, 290, 300, 310, 320) stitches. We used a basic Long Tail Cast On.

Knit every row until you have 40 (45, 50, 54, 58, 63) garter stitch ridges [see Notes, above].

Divide fronts and back

Bind off 90 (90, 95, 95, 95, 95) stitches for Left Front, knit until there are 80 (90, 100, 110, 120, 130) stitches on right needle for Back, join second ball of yarn and bind off remaining 90 (90, 95, 95, 95, 95) stitches for Right Front. Cut the yarn and pull it through the remaining stitch.

Continue back

Knit every row over center 80 (90, 100, 110, 120, 130) stitches until you have 81 (81, 85, 85, 85, 85) garter ridges from the bind-off rows.

Bind off all stitches. Cut yarn and pull it through the remaining stitch.

Sleeves

Note: Make two identical sleeves.

Cast on 60 (60, 66, 66, 66, 66) stitches.

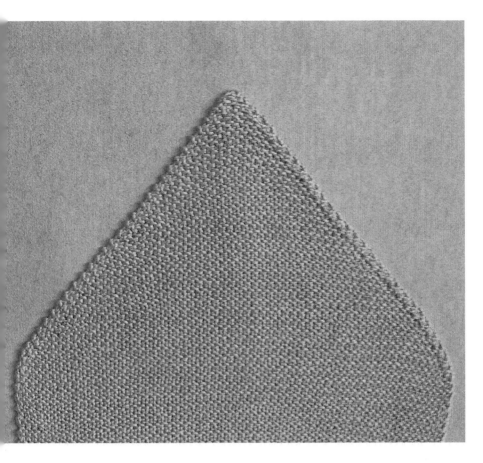

Knit every row until you have 30 (30, 33, 33, 33, 33) garter ridges.

Row 1 (right side): K1, slip 1, k1, psso (pass slipped stitch over), knit to last 2 stitches, slip stitch just worked back to left needle and pass second-to-last stitch over and off needle, slip stitch back to right needle, knit last stitch. [2 stitches decreased]

Row 2: Knit.

Repeat Rows 1 and 2 until 4 stitches remain.

Next Row (right side): K1, k2tog, k1. [3 stitches]

Next Row: K1, k2tog. [2 stitches]

Next Row: k2tog. [1 stitch]

Cut yarn and pull it through last stitch.

Finish

Weave in ends and block all three pieces. Block by submerging them fully in water, gently squeezing out the excess water, and laying them flat to dry (shaping to finished measurements).

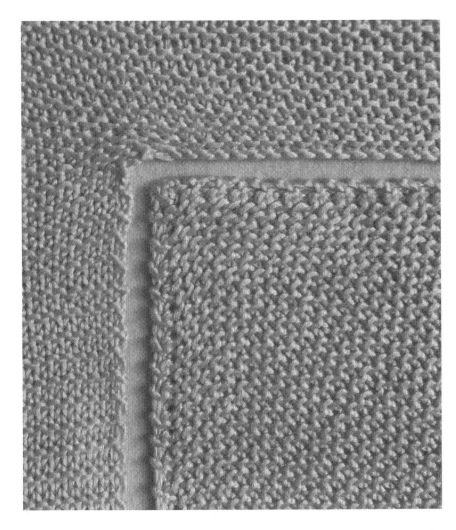

With the wrong sides facing up, position the top points of each Sleeve under each side of the "T," as shown in the schematic in the Notes section, above.

Starting at the base of one Sleeve point, whipstitch the Sleeve's top point to the underside of the T-shape, shown in the schematic as a bold line.

Sew the Sleeve's underside seams together. For tips, visit our Seaming

Garter Stitch Tutorial.

Fold the Cardigan along the schematic's dotted lines and whipstitch the body's side seams to finish.

Weave in the ends and enjoy your Folded Squares Cardigan!

Made in United States
Troutdale, OR
11/08/2024